Birthday Party

By Diane Church

Photographs by Chris Fairclough

W

FRANKLIN WATTS
LONDON • SYDNEY

Alex and Ruby are best friends.
They play together all the time.
Alex has a food allergy.
She is allergic to nuts.
This means that if she eats
anything with nuts in it she
becomes very ill.

Today is Alex's birthday.
She is seven and she's having
a party to celebrate.

People can be allergic to many different things including eggs, milk, fish and sesame seeds. If you have an allergy it is important to be very careful what you eat and to tell your friends.

Ruby arrives early. "Happy birthday!" she says and gives Alex a present. "Thank you very much, Ruby," says Alex. "Come in and help us get ready!"

First they are going shopping so they make a list. "Shall we get some cakes?" Alex asks her mum. "And some balloons too!" says Alex's brother, Miles.

People with nut allergies need to be careful that any food they buy does not contain nuts or any product made from nuts.

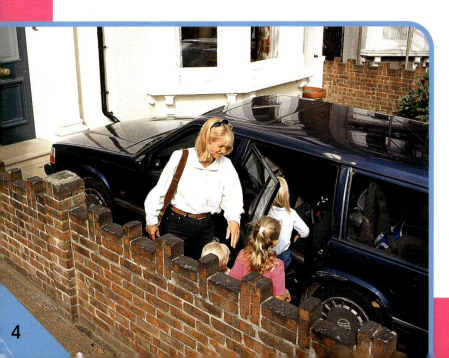

"What about some crisps and biscuits?" Ruby asks as they all get into the car.

4

At the supermarket, the girls go to the bakery. "Can you eat doughnuts?" Ruby asks. "No, I'm not allowed anything from here," explains Alex. "We could make some cakes at home instead," suggests Ruby.

Some of the bread and cakes at the bakery have nuts in them. So Alex can't eat anything from the bakery at all just in case a nut has got into the other cakes or bread by mistake.

As they go around the shop, Alex's mum carefully checks the labels on the food. "Can you see the label on this one?" she asks Alex and Ruby.

"When we get back we'll make the cakes," Alex chatters excitedly as they load the car. "I hope my friends remember not to bring anything with nuts in!"

Some people wear a special bracelet that says they have an allergy. Alex doesn't wear one so she has to remember to tell everyone about her allergy to nuts.

At home, they gather together all the ingredients they need to make the cakes. "We can have some with chocolate and some with cherries," says Alex.

Alex isn't only allergic to eating nuts. Touching a nut could be enough to cause an allergic reaction, so she has to keep well away from them.

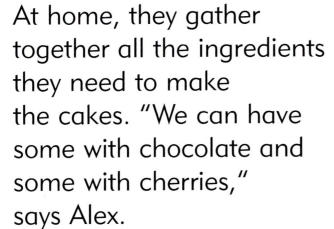

While the cakes cook, Alex and Ruby play in the bedroom. "What would happen if you ate a nut?" Ruby asks. "I'd have an allergic reaction which means I'd be really unwell," Alex tells her. "But I've got this special kit that helps me."

If Alex ate nuts, her body would react badly. Her skin would become red and her mouth and throat would swell up, making it hard for her to breathe.

"If I had a bad allergic reaction, I'd have this injection in my leg," Alex explains as she shows Ruby the injection kit. "I've seen you with your kit at school, too," says Ruby.

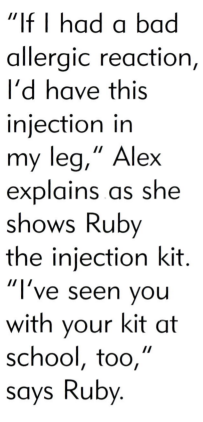

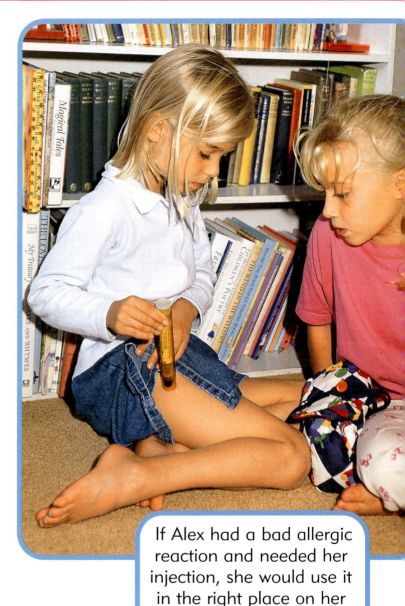

People with allergies may carry a special injection kit which could save their lives. Alex makes sure hers is always nearby. She also has a spare one at school.

If Alex had a bad allergic reaction and needed her injection, she would use it in the right place on her leg. Here she is practising with her kit which is still in its case.

It's soon time for the girls to get ready! They put on their party dresses. "I really like your dress, Ruby," Alex tells her friend.

Next Alex and Ruby blow up lots of balloons and get the birthday banner.

Then Ella and Louis arrive. "Happy birthday!" they say. Louis is wearing his batman outfit.
"I like your costume," Ruby tells him.

Alex opens her presents.
"Thank you, that's
brilliant," she cries.
Ella has given her a
cuddly toy. "He's
gorgeous!" Alex says.

Ella has also given Alex some sweets. But Alex cannot eat this variety because they may have nuts in them. "I'm sure my Mum will like them though!" giggles Alex.

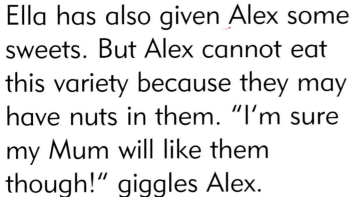

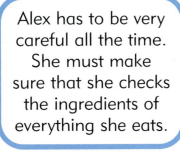
Alex has to be very careful all the time. She must make sure that she checks the ingredients of everything she eats.

Everyone has fun playing in the
garden. "Throw the ball to me!"
laughs Louis.

"Tea's ready!" calls Ella's mum. The children sit at the table and tuck into the party food.
"Yummy!" says Miles.

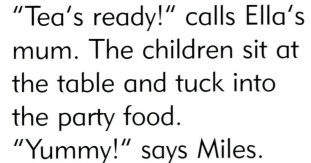

Alex's home is a nut free zone so she doesn't have to worry about any of the food on the table. She can try everything!

There are lots of different things
to eat. "I really like these
cakes," says Louis.
"We made them!" Alex
and Ruby tell him.

"And now it's time for the cake," says Alex's mum. She lights the candles and everyone bursts into song, "Happy birthday to you..."

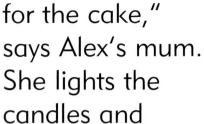
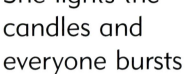

Alex takes a deep breath and blows the candles out.
"What did you wish for?" asks Ruby.
"If I tell you it won't come true!" Alex laughs.

After tea, it's time for Ruby, Ella and Louis to go home. They wave goodbye. "Thanks for a great party!" says Ruby. "See you soon!" calls Alex.

Facts about people with food allergies

 ⭐ One child in 200 has a nut allergy: that's a lot of children!

 ⭐ The symptoms range from a mild rash to a serious allergic reaction called anaphylaxis.

 ⭐ One of the most common form of food allergies is to nuts: peanuts, walnuts, almonds, brazil nuts and hazel nuts.

 ⭐ An allergic reaction can be treated with the right medicines.

 ⭐ Some people are allergic to bee and wasp stings, pulses (beans and lentils); or dairy products (milk, cheese, yogurt, butter), fish, eggs or even rubber.

Glossary

Anaphylaxis When the body suffers a very bad allergic reaction. If a person with anaphylaxis does not take their medicine or get immediate medical help, they could die. Symptoms may include difficulty in breathing, swelling around the throat and tongue, difficulty in speaking and swallowing, floppiness or stillness. Some children may be sick or pass out. Children do not need to experience all of these symptoms to be at risk.

Injection kit An injection kit has a pen which contains an adrenaline injection inside its tube. If Alex had a bad allergic reaction she would push the tube against her leg and hold it there for ten seconds. After this she should be fine but she must still go to hospital.

Try to be helpful

★ **1.** Do your best to stop someone with an allergy from eating that type of food. Think hard about all the products that may contain that food, it isn't always obvious. For example, did you know that marzipan is made with nuts ?

★ **2.** If someone reacts badly to a food or an insect sting, tell an adult. The person may need their emergency injection kit. Call 999 for an ambulance.

★ **3.** Make sure that you are able to recognise the symptoms of a food allergy and know what to do if someone needs help.

★ **4.** If you're not sure if something you are eating has nuts in it, don't offer to share it with a person who is allergic.

★ **5.** Remember having a food allergy doesn't stop you having fun!

Further information and addresses

Here is a list of useful organisations if you require further support or information:

The Anaphylaxis Campaign
The Ridges, 2 Clockhouse Road
Farnborough, Hampshire GU14 7QY
Helpline: 01252 542 029
E-mail: info@www.anaphylaxis.org.uk
www.anaphylaxis.org.uk

Allergy UK
Deepdene House
30 Bellgrove Road
Kent DA16 3PY
Email: info@allergyfoundation.com
www.allergyfoundation.com

National Centre for Language and Literacy
Bulmershe Court, Earley
Reading RG6 1HY
E-mail: ncll@reading.ac.uk

Food Anaphylactic Children Training and Support (FACTS)
21 Robinson Close, Hornsbury Heights
NSW 2077
Australia
www.allergyfacts.org.au

Index

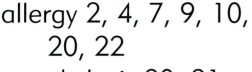

This edition 2003

Franklin Watts
96 Leonard Street
London
EC2A 4XD

Franklin Watts Australia
45-51 Huntley Street
Alexandria
NSW 2015

© 2000 Franklin Watts

ISBN: 0 7496 5184 9

Dewey Decimal Classification
Number: 362.4

A CIP catalogue record for
this book is available from the
British Library.

Printed in Malaysia

Consultants: The Anaphylaxis Campaign;
Beverley Mathias, REACH.
Editor: Samantha Armstrong
Designer: Louise Snowdon
Photographer: Chris Fairclough
Illustrator: Eliz Hüseyin

With thanks to: Alex Kellock and her family,
Ruby and Ella Gurdon and Louis Fox, Tesco at
Brixton, South London and The Anaphylaxis
Campaign.